BTS

K-POP'S INTERNATIONAL SUPERSTARS

KATY SPRINKEL

TRIUMPH
BOOKS

This book is available in quantity at special discounts for your group or organization. For further information, contact:

Triumph Books LLC
814 North Franklin Street
Chicago, Illinois 60610
(312) 337–0747
www.triumphbooks.com

Printed in U.S.A.

ISBN: 978-1-62937-636-3

Content written, developed, and packaged by
   Katy Sprinkel
Edited by Laine Morreau
Design and page production by Patricia Frey
Cover design by Preston Pisellini

Images on pages 1, 18, 28, 30, 31, 33, 43, 75, and 101 courtesy of AP Images. Images on pages 3, 4, 8, 11, 12, 13, 14, 15, 17, 21, 24, 27, 34, 37, 40, 46, 49, 50, 54, 56, 59, 60, 63, 64, 67, 68, 71, 72, 76, 79, 80, 83, 86, 96, 103, 104, 107, 108, 111, and 112 courtesy of Getty Images.

CHAPTER ONE

THE BIRTH OF COOL

BT WHO?

You might not have heard of them—yet—but Billboard has. BTS has had two songs chart on the Billboard Hot 100 singles list, are the highest-charting Asian artist *ever* on the Billboard 200 albums chart, and ruled Billboard's Social 50 chart for all but seven weeks in 2017—and all of 2018...so far. They've also already graced *Billboard* magazine's cover (actually, seven of them—one cover for each of BTS's seven members). In June 2018, they became the first ever group who doesn't record primarily in English to hit No. 1 on the Artists 100 as the top-selling artist in the U.S. What's more, they have a devoted legion of fans who earned them the Top Social Artist award at the Billboard Music Awards in 2017 and 2018, besting the likes of Justin Bieber, Ariana Grande, Selena Gomez, and Shawn Mendes.

And while Billboard statistics are all fine and good, they don't tell anywhere near the full story of BTS. Already breaking the mold in the hugely successful genre of K-pop, BTS is a crossover success in the States. Why?

Their unique brand of socially conscious pop/hip-hop music, slick choreography, and unprecedented fan engagement has set them apart from the rest of their contemporaries. Their self-dubbed "ARMY" of fans is a force to be reckoned with.

Formed in 2013, BTS (aka the Bangtan Boys, Bangtan Sonyeondan, the Bullet-proof Boy Scouts, and the more recent moniker Beyond the Scene) is a seven-man band consisting of rappers RM, Suga, and J-Hope and vocalists Jin, V, Jimin, and Jungkook. Together, the multitalented Bangtan Boys have seamlessly blended their talents to create a unique K-pop group. Focusing on issues beyond the typical dance-pop offerings, BTS struck a chord with fans.

Let's get one thing straight first: BTS is no fly-by-night operation. They are nothing less than international superstars. Since making their debut in 2013 they've been absolutely *killing* it in their native South Korea—they're the best-selling musical group in the country and have won Korea's top artist prize for the last two years running. (They've also hit No. 1 in 72 other countries, thank you very much.)

They're the face of several brands, including Puma, Gonsen (cosmetics), and LG Electronics. They're also representing another well-known brand—Coca-Cola, anyone?—at the 2018 World Cup, perhaps the world's biggest advertising stage. With *Love Yourself: Tear* reaching even greater heights, BTS is poised to take America by storm.

BY THE NUMBERS 4.7 BILLION

According to the Korea Creative Content Agency, K-pop revenues in 2016, including marketing and licensing, earned more than $4.7 billion in total revenues. That's a pretty penny!

But first, a little history. To the outside observer, K-pop looks like a sugarcoated confection, a frenetic collection of beats, catchy hooks, super-sharp dancing, and kaleidoscopic visuals performed by impossibly attractive singers and entertainers. But to dismiss it as a cotton-candy version of pop music would be way off the mark. Not only is K-pop wide-ranging in its musical styles and onstage product, it's serious business. Big business.

In fact, it is nearly impossible to overestimate the power of K-pop. The multibillion-dollar industry (that's right, *billion* with a *B*) is one of South Korea's biggest exports, and a huge contributor to the country's bottom line. Those eye-

"THERE MAY BE NO MORE UNLIKELY POP-CULTURE SUCCESS IN THE WORLD RIGHT NOW THAN SOUTH KOREAN HALLYU."—WALL STREET JOURNAL

popping numbers are pretty impressive for a country with a population of only 51 million. (Compare that to the U.S.'s 326 million.) In fact, South Korea "is the world's eighth-largest market for recorded music by revenue, according to the International Federation of the Phonographic Industry," Bloomberg reports. What's more, that's bigger than India (whose own entertainment industry is well-known worldwide) and even China. (And for those of you doing the math, India and China are the two most populous countries in the world, with more than 1.3 *billion* citizens apiece.)

So how did Korean culture become so pervasive? Let's rewind to the mid-20th century. In the aftermath of the Korean War, the country's ruler, dictator Park Chung-hee, enforced strict cultural conservatism. (This included such "standards" as enforcing short haircuts on men and modest hemlines on women's clothing.) Additionally, the government controlled the media, so all radio and television programming was under its purview. The end result in music was an especially bland mixture of inoffensive,

GREAT MOMENTS IN HALLYU

In just a short span of time, South Korea has become the entertainment capital of Asia. Here's a look back at how they got there.

1986: Censorship laws are repealed, allowing for greater artistic freedom across the entire entertainment industry.

1988: Foreign travel ban is lifted by the South Korean government, allowing tourism to flourish.

1999: Korea-set spy thriller *Swiri* is released.

2000: *Autumn in My Heart* is released.

2002: *Winter Sonata* premieres in Japan; a nation is riveted.

2012: Psy's "Gangnam Style" becomes the first video to eclipse 1 billion views on YouTube.

2012: The K-pop festival KCON begins, staging a first show in Irvine, California. That first concert draws 20,000 fans.

2012: Samsung becomes the best-selling mobile phone maker in the world.

2016: The Korean smash hit *My Love from Another Star* premieres in China after censors finally relax their restrictions on the K-drama.

2017: KCON plays to 85,000 at L.A.'s Staples Center, and more than 40,000 outside New York City—and those are just the U.S. shows!

2018: The world's attention turns to South Korea, host of the 2018 Winter Olympics. Many K-pop acts and other entertainers are featured throughout the festivities.

Coming Soon: Hooray for Hallyu-wood! The theme park will soon open to K-fanatics worldwide.

by-the-numbers pop music alongside traditional Korean music, known as *trot* (short for *foxtrot*).

When South Korea became a democracy in 1987, things started to relax a little bit. One of the most popular television formats in South Korea at that time (and today), is the musical competition show. Forebears to Western programs such as *American Idol* and *The X Factor*, Korea's weekly music shows—such as *Inkigayo* and *Music Bank*—were nothing less than appointment television. (And in a country where 99 percent of homes had a TV, that's saying something.) Audiences were (and remain) hugely invested in the outcomes.

Enter Seo Taiji and the Boys. On April 11, 1992, the trio performed on the MBC network's weekly talent show. Their song, "Nan Arayo" ("I Know") contained lots of elements that would have been familiar to Americans at that time but were wholly unfamiliar to local audiences. It was seemingly influenced by the new jack swing style popularized by groups Bell Biv DeVoe and Bobby Brown, among others, in the early 1990s. The unusual performance rocked the panel—but not in a good way. Seo Taiji and the Boys received the lowest possible rating from the judges. The band didn't win the competition, or even the day, but they did something far more lasting. They lit the spark that ignited the K-pop explosion. Their performance had a ripple effect on musicians who began to expand their sound beyond the predictable, staid formula popular in South Korea at the time. Unequivocally, this 1992 performance is considered to be the official beginning of K-pop as we know it today.

VOCAB

bang song
(broadcast)

Meaning *broadcast*, it refers to the weekly music shows that are hugely influential in shaping the Korean musical landscape.

THEY CALL IT HALLYU—THE
KOREAN WAVE—AND IT DESCRIBES
THE INFLUENCE OF KOREAN
CULTURE ON CONSUMERS.

BTS performs on the
MBC Music program
Show Champion.

Psy performs his smash "Gangnam Style" in Rockefeller Plaza for a *Today* broadcast in 2012.

When the Asian financial crisis swept across the continent in 1997, South Korea appeared to be on the brink of bankruptcy. Then-president Kim Dae-jung made a bold move, investing heavily in South Korea's entertainment industry as a means of saving the country from collapse. The gambit worked.

Korean music became popular in China as soon as it hit the airwaves there. And when Korean shows landed on Japanese television screens, viewers couldn't get enough. International audiences' obsession with Korean entertainers had an enormous ripple effect, and the craze for all things Korean became all-encompassing.

They call it *hallyu*—the Korean wave—and it describes the influence of Korean culture on consumers. It encompasses not just music but television and movies, business, fashion, beauty, and even cuisine. (It sounds outlandish, but it's not inaccurate to say that the international rise in popularity of K-pop and Korean television (K-drama) has created opportunities for people around the world to buy Samsung phones

POP QUIZ

Q: What's considered the epicenter of *hallyu* culture?

A: That's right, it's the Gangnam district of Seoul, as Psy made popular in his 2012 song "Gangnam Style."

and get kimchi at their local grocery stores.) The term was initially coined by Chinese journalists looking to describe the immense effect Korean culture was having on Chinese pop culture. The word was subsequently adopted by the South Korean government as a badge of honor and a tool for promoting both industry and tourism.

Today, the wave of *hallyu* is stronger than ever. But despite K-pop's giant popularity in Japan, China, and places as far-flung as Brazil, Australia, and

Mexico, the music has still not seen a major breakthrough in the U.S. (Except for outlier Psy, whose 2012 smash "Gangnam Style" was a record-breaking commercial success but is now relegated to a footnote at best, a novelty song at worst.)

If any act seems poised to finally crack the U.S. market, it is BTS. Their fan base is young, energetic, and millions strong. What's more, the band has serious musical street cred and has already collaborated with hugely successful U.S. artists, from the Chainsmokers and Fall Out Boy to Steve Aoki and hip-hop OG Warren G. Though they have yet to release an all-English-language album, it was reported in November 2017 that BTS had signed with a subsidiary label of Sony Music, which will promote them in the States, a huge signal that a U.S. push is in the works.

Get ready, ARMY: the Korean invasion is coming to America, and BTS is leading the charge. 끝

BTS at KCON 2014
in Los Angeles.

CHAPTER TWO

THE K-POP MACHINE

Seo Taiji and the Boys might not have received immediate acclaim for their innovation, but no one could say they didn't get attention. Their performance was something completely and utterly new, and it polarized audiences, who had never before seen a mash-up of Korean and American music. They were sharply criticized by some who objected to their use of hip-hop beats and rhythms (now the stock in trade of K-pop). They also committed such unforgivable sins as sporting dreadlocked hair and wearing bleached and ripped jeans.

Despite such trespasses, the song "Nan Arayo" ultimately became a huge hit at home—it reigned for 17 weeks as the No. 1 song in the country—and Seo Taiji and the Boys established themselves as a massive idol group. They rode a tidal wave of success in the following four years, all the while experimenting with a wide range of musical styles, from hip-hop and rap styles popular over the American airwaves at that time to the softer, sweeter R&B balladeering of U.S. artists such as K-Ci & JoJo and Babyface.

The reason why they are considered the first K-pop band is that they literally blew up the system. In general, fans don't really consider K-pop to be a genre of music because there's no one identifiable sound. Korean groups are extremely open to experimentation and changing their sound, mashing up different influences. It's all about the full experience: the music, the live performance, the videos, the variety/competition shows, and the physical packaging of the musical product. Before Seo Taiji and the Boys, music was ostensibly minted by the broadcasting companies who promoted their own on-air products. But this group wrote, produced, and choreographed everything on their own. And because of their success, they upended the status quo. A new studio production company system was born.

When the band broke up in 1996, one of the "Boys"—Yang Hyun-suk—joined the fray, founding YG Entertainment. (The YG comes from his nickname, Yang-gun.) The YG agency is one of the so-called "Big Three" entertainment companies in Korea. Along with JYP Entertainment and SM Entertainment (which were also founded by former musicians), they dominate the musical landscape in Korea. Together, they produce the lion's share of K-pop music, and their reach is enormous.

Ask any K-pop fan, and they could tell you about each label's hallmarks. Listeners are loyal to their chosen label, much as sports fans stay true to their team's colors. Since its inception in 1995, SM has been the leader of the pack. Home to hundreds of artists, it's known for its performance-oriented focus (big visuals, sharp choreography, and catchy, danceable tunes are its focus). JYP is

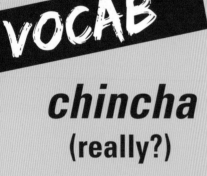

VOCAB

chincha
(really?)

As in, "Did you hear that BTS was nominated this year for four Radio Disney Awards?" "*Chincha?* That's awesome!"

From clothing to choreography, the members of Girls' Generation are in sync.

The scene from KCON 2016 in Paris.

known for its polished trainee program and diverse class of recruits, turning out some of the most well-rounded musicians of the bunch. YG, like its founder, produces artists who tend to push musical barriers and who possess an edgier look than their competitors.

Rather than focusing on grooming a select number of artists for long-term success, these companies churn out a multitude of acts, a seemingly revolving door for bands. The metrics for success are simply different in the K-pop system, where a band's shelf life may only be two years. This span is dictated by a couple things: First, the emphasis on youth. Since image is an essential component of the K-pop look, many artists age out of the system quickly. And for boy groups, things are also complicated by age. All male citizens in South Korea must serve two years in the military, entering a draft at age 18.

Performers start early, auditioning as young as 9 or 10 years old. Foreign language fluency is prized in trainees, and native English speakers are a sought-after commodity. Once individuals are recruited by an agency and signed to long-term contracts, their formal training begins. Children are schooled during the day—a curriculum that includes a heavy dose of foreign language training, particularly Chinese, Japanese, and English. Then, once the school day is over, students start their music training—singing, dancing, and even media training. This is not for the faint of heart; a typical day begins early in the morning and stretches until 8:00 or 9:00 p.m., before students return to their dormitories to complete their day's homework.

The performers will spend years as trainees before they are finally brought to market, only premiering once they

PERFORMERS START EARLY, AUDITIONING AS YOUNG AS 9 OR 10 YEARS OLD.

KNOW YOUR IDOLS

Here are a handful of artists from K-pop's glittering past.

G.O.D.

One of the earliest K-pop groups, g.o.d (Groove Over Dose) remains one of the genre's best-selling artists.

Recommended listening: "Lies"

BOA

The Korean Queen of Pop's multilingual chops made her a bona fide international success.

Recommended listening: "Valenti"

S.E.S.

The first successful girl group of the K-pop era, S.E.S. (taking its initials from members Sea (Bada), Eugene, and Shoo) traded their good-girl image for a more provocative look over the years.

Recommended listening: "I'm Your Girl"

Kim Yoo-jin (Eugene)
of S.E.S.

RAIN

Solo artist and actor Rain became one of K-pop's first international success stories.

Recommended listening: "Rainism"

WONDER GIRLS

They made a splash in the U.S., opening on tour for the Jonas Brothers and scoring a Billboard 100 hit in 2009.

Recommended listening: "Nobody"

SUPER JUNIOR

K-pop's "biggest" group has had as many as 13 members over the years.

Recommended listening: "Mr. Simple"

GIRLS' GENERATION

The female counterpart to Super Junior, the nine members of Girls' Generation write their own music.

Recommended listening: "Gee"

BIG BANG

The so-called "Kings of K-pop," composed of members T.O.P., Taeyang, G-Dragon, Daesung, and Seungri, have found heated competition in BTS.

Recommended listening: "Bang Bang Bang"

have mastered their performances down to every hand gesture and eye wink. No detail is overlooked. But the breakneck pace doesn't let up any after their debut. Groups tour extensively, promote exhaustively, and are often tabbed for endorsement deals that require appearances and other promotional efforts. As Tiffany Chan writes on Medium.com, "These South Korean stars represent much more than their latest album…they uphold the image of an ideal in South Korean society, perfectly in-sync choreography, strong vocal talent, and exceptionally attractive visuals."

The companies also take charge of creating and distributing fan chants, which are another essential part of the live shows. Fans will have what amounts to a script. Instead of vocal backing tracks, live performances are enhanced by precisely crafted audience chants. Most songs have them, and it makes regular callbacks look like child's play. (Case in point: the stuff of BTS's fan chants are disseminated, discussed, and practiced exhaustively by ARMYs.)

THE GLOBAL SHIFT IN THE MUSIC INDUSTRY IN THE INFORMATION AGE HAS BEEN A HUGE PART OF K-POP'S MODERN-DAY SUCCESS STORY.

Then there's the music. Groups are expected to release songs early and often. In contrast to the American record industry, groups announce their releases a few weeks in advance, drop the EP or album, then start the process all over again. Typically, a K-pop group will release music throughout the calendar year.

And that music is almost always accompanied by a music video, an integral part of the K-pop formula. These videos are invariably lavishly produced affairs that feature the requisite come-hither stares from idol group members but also showcase the groups' onstage prowess. The past two decades gave rise to countless idol groups, to whom BTS owes tribute.

The global shift in the music industry in the Information age has been a huge part of K-pop's modern-day success story, which is fueled in large part by the Internet. No artist saw greater proof of that than Psy, whose humorous video for "Gangnam Style" set seemingly unsurpassable records on the streaming site, reaching 1 billion views in record time to become the most-watched video by a huge margin. Six years later, with YouTube *the* undisputed platform for accessing music videos, it's still the fourth-most-watched video of all time.

Given the establishment in the K-pop industry, BTS's success has been shocking—they have long been considered an underdog group since they were recruited under the Big Hit Entertainment umbrella as opposed to by one of the Big Three. Undoubtedly, the Internet has played a central role in their ascent. Their online popularity is unprecedented, and that has everything to do with their fan base. As *Dazed* magazine put it, "They may still be regarded as an overnight phenomenon by an American media...but even the tiniest peek behind the glittery curtain shows how ferociously BTS have dedicated themselves to nurturing a long-term symbiotic relationship between the group and their fandom."

Their wide-ranging talents, along with the fervency of their ARMY, have taken them to the top of the heap both in South Korea and abroad. And they show no signs of stopping. 끝

THE BIG THREE VS. BIG HIT

The Bangtan Boys and their agency, Big Hit Entertainment, are giving the Big Three a run for their money.

	SM Entertainment	YG Entertainment	JYP Entertainment	Big Hit Entertainment
Founder	Lee Soo-man	Yang Hyun-suk	Park Jin-young	Bang Si-hyuk
Operating since	1995	1996	1997	2005
Known for	Strict training regimen	Songwriting	Culturally and musically diverse artists	Allowing their flagship group, BTS, to have total artistic freedom
Biggest acts	S.E.S., H.O.T., Shinee, Girls' Generation, BoA, EXO, Super Junior	Big Bang, Blackpink, iKON, 2NE1	TWICE, 2PM, Wonder Girls, Rain, Miss A, San E	BTS, Homme, Lee Hyun
Milestone	Has long ruled as the No. 1 agency, with huge stable of artists, but has yet to substantially break into the U.S. market	Psy's "Gangnam Style" becomes an international phenomenon	TWICE and former Miss A member Suzy propel the agency to No. 2 in earnings among the Big Three	BTS shakes up the establishment, becoming a phenomenon at home and abroad
Also dabbles in...	Film, TV, theater, and even a travel agency	TV, apparel, cosmetics, and sports	Film, TV, restaurants, games, and even operates a business school	None

CHAPTER THREE

AN ARMY RISES

The year was 2010. Big Hit Entertainment was still looking for...well, a big hit. They had a promising recruit in Rap Monster (aka RM), but they thought he might fit better into an idol group. Members were scouted through various auditions and brought into the agency's fold as trainees. The roster fluctuated a bit in those early training years, but once Jimin joined in 2013, the ensemble was set: RM, J-Hope, Suga, Jimin, V, Jin, and Jungkook were Bangtan Sonyeondan—translating roughly to the Bulletproof Boy Scouts and better known as BTS.

They made their official debut in June 2013, releasing their first single, "No More Dream," from the *2 Cool 4 Skool* EP. It was a daring debut that boldly challenged the South Korean status quo. The release earned them a number of Best New Artist awards in South Korea, including Golden Disk and Seoul Music Awards honors.

From there, the band was off and running, releasing EP after EP at breakneck speed. A short three years later, they had the best-selling album in Korea's history and were selling out arenas across the globe.

Little by little, they have started to make inroads in America. Streaming sites such as YouTube have made all the difference. Gone are the days of radio play and MTV; in the Internet age it's all about streaming. "Right now young people both discover and enjoy music on YouTube for free and with great ease—either via laptops or mobiles," reported the *Daily Telegraph*. "It has become both the MTV and CD shop for teenage music-lovers." In fact, according to a recent Nielsen study, nearly two-thirds of 18-year-olds and younger U.S. teens say that they prefer YouTube ahead of all other music mediums.

This has been a crucial advantage for K-pop, according to experts in the industry, who first saw the genre's views skyrocket from 2 billion to 7 billion in the wake of "Gangnam Style." "It might have been impossible for K-pop to have worldwide popularity without YouTube's global platform," Sun Lee, head of music partnerships for Korea and Greater China at YouTube and Google Play, told Bloomberg. "K-pop is creating a great sensation in the U.S."

And it's not just YouTube. Playlists—which three-quarters of online music listeners create, share, or otherwise listen to, and which more than half consider important to their listening experience—have helped introduce BTS to listeners stateside. Spotify said that streams of Korean music doubled in the first half of 2017, and that listeners in the U.S. made up one-quarter of that audience. (Speaking of Spotify, you can listen to personalized playlists curated by each of the Bangtan Boys on their BTS channel.)

VOCAB

daesang
(top award)

As in, "BTS won their first *daesang* in 2016, nabbing the Melon Music Award for their album *Young Forever*."

COMMUNIQUES FROM THE ARMY

"Their amazing choreography and the hip hop vibe is why I became a big fanboy of bts."—Matt Spencer via YouTube

"I DON'T WANT YOU TO CHANGE. I don't want you to sing in english with other people and change your special style, I wouldn't like you to be one more like those 'american artists.' You are BTS, I fell in love with your singing skills, your dancing, your different personality, your MV, and your talent. Please... Don't ever let anyone change you."—Freddie Goldstein via Facebook

"BTS's dedication, their talent, and lyrics set them apart. They worked so hard to get where they are, and they remain humble through all of it."—Carlen Wirth to the author

"Their message is beyond just making good music. They talk about social issues. They stand for more than your typical boy band would stand for. I think that's really important for people my age and the younger generation to really understand. Everything on social media, you kind of get desensitized to everything out there. But BTS brings it to the forefront…. That really sets them apart for me in comparison to anyone else out in the industry."—Christine Gee to *Billboard* magazine

"The world's BEST athletes, entertainers, and ARTISTS" #NoPrinterJustFax #BTSDIDTHAT #WORLDWIDESTARS #INTERNTATIONALPLAYBOYS"
—@BTS_ARMY_INT via Twitter

"[BTS is] a symbol, in a way, that the world doesn't have to be so far apart. We're actually really close together."—Sara Donis to *Billboard* magazine

"Our boys teach us to be kind with others and spread a lot of love in order to finish the hate."—Alejandra Tarazona via Buzzfeed message board

"these boys…I AM SO PROUD OF THEM i am really happy that i stan these 7 beautiful souls they deserve everything we will love&support them forever"—@panaceabangtan via Twitter

"They do not try to impress anybody just to be on top. They don't make music just to be popular they make it to connect to people."—Euphoria via AminoApps ARMY's group

"I am so excited to see other moms loving BTS! I always feel too old, but I am totally obsessed!… BTS has just been an inspiration to me. They have been helping getting me out [of] my depression….it would be so nice to one day get to see them live. <3 #ThankyouBTS"—Grace Kan-Tanabe via Facebook

"BTS choosing to release songs in Korean while breaking out in the West with these songs is a prime example that it is possible for your music and content to be loved without the need to completely assimilate to other cultures or languages…. [BTS is] a talented and amazing group of artists in a class of their own."—@BangtanUAE to *Nylon* magazine

CELEBS LOVE BTS TOO!

Turns out celebrities are stans just like the rest of us. The band's fans in Hollywood include: Ansel Elgort, Demi Lovato, Perez Hilton, the Chainsmokers, Halsey, Wale, Charli XCX, Camila Cabello, Charlie Puth, Major Lazer, Zedd, Jared Leto, Shawn Mendes, Tyra Banks, Laura Marano, DNCE, Marshmello, Khalid, and John Cena, among others!

All that online buzz has combined to create a fan base that is young, Internet-savvy, and extremely motivated. Consider that as of this writing, BTS's official Twitter has "only" 15 million followers, yet those followers made BTS the most retweeted Twitter account in 2017—more than Donald Trump and Justin Bieber (with their 51 million and 106 million followers, respectively) *combined*. They established a Guinness World Record in 2018 as the music act with the most Twitter engagements.

The success comes from their unique brand of K-pop, certainly. But the effect that their fans have had on their rise cannot be understated. And for BTS, fan power is a highly utilized resource. Fans are treated to a personal side of their idols and engage with them directly in a way most artists do not. BTS posts around the clock—from candid videos and messages to produced content such as YouTube Red's recent documentary series *BTS: Burn the Stage*. If you're following BTS, you know it all.

Their fan base, the ARMY, an acronym for Adorable Representative MC for Youth, has done everything it can possibly do to make sure its idols get their due.

"The BTS ARMY…is the engine powering the phenomenon," reports *Billboard* magazine. "It translates lyrics and Korean media appearances; rallies clicks, views, likes and retweets to get BTS trending on Twitter and YouTube; and overwhelms online polls and competitions. Big Hit says that it makes sure to disseminate news and updates about the band on the fan cafe, so as not to arouse the wrath of the ARMY."

The ARMY was there to hand the band their first win on the prestigious Korean music competition *Inkigayo* in 2016 by goosing the band's digital sales numbers to help put them over the top. They were there again when the band simultaneously hit No. 1 on all eight of the Korean charts (an "all-kill") with "Blood, Sweat & Tears." And they were there to elevate the band's album sales and YouTube views to levels never before seen by a Korean idol group.

In the U.S., BTS *owns* Billboard's Social 50 chart. They've been at No. 1 for a year and a half at last tally. The band also took home the Billboard Music Award for Top Social Artist in 2017, becoming the first Korean artist ever to win a BBMA. They won again in 2018, with even more ARMYs in attendance to celebrate. (BBMA host Kelly Clarkson wore noise-canceling headphones when she introduced them for their onstage performance.)

They hit *Time*'s Top 25 Most Influential People on the Internet list in 2017. And when the magazine reached out to readers to ask who should be included in its annual Time 100 list, the ARMY

FOLLOWERS MADE BTS'S THE MOST RETWEETED TWITTER ACCOUNT IN 2017—MORE THAN DONALD TRUMP'S AND JUSTIN BIEBER'S COMBINED.

was there too. They made BTS the No. 1 vote-getter, by a margin almost ten times more than the closest competitor. It's little wonder that they're considered Korea's No. 1 Power Celebrity, according to *Forbes*. As industry analyst Jason Joven put it, "The BTS ARMY, empowered by their freedom from close-minded stereotypes of Asian artists and a diligent mastery of digital coordination, simply brings fandom to another level."

That immensity is not lost on the band, who constantly thank their fans for their support and inspiration. "I… attribute the glory to all of our ARMYs," Jin told *Billboard* after the band hit the Hot 100 for the first time. "I think that even if you make music, you need people to listen to it in order to climb up. I'm always grateful to ARMYs and love them."

ARMYs have time and again proven their devotion to their chosen idol group, but what's often overlooked is their devotion to one another. It's not unusual to see ARMYs standing up for one another or sending each other messages of encouragement or kinship.

DID YOU KNOW?

BTS is the first (and still only) K-pop group to have its own Twitter emoji. The social media site created a special emoji for the band: a bulletproof vest emblazoned with the letters BTS befitting the Bulletproof Boy Scouts themselves!

They truly are a family unto themselves, and a globally connected community of disparate personalities.

Bringing people together is indeed one of the greatest achievements BTS has had so far in their still-blossoming career. Across the generations and the miles, they have cultivated a fan base that embraces not only love for the band but for one another. 끝

CHAPTER FOUR

MEET THE BANGTAN BOYS

I mean, sure, the ARMY loves all things BTS—the music, the message, the slick videos, the killer choreography. But we can't forget the band's most important asset—well, seven most important, really. For the uninitiated, consider this your formal introduction.

RM

The discussion has to start with the leader of the group and its first member, RM (formerly Rap Monster). He started out as an underground rapper, making a name for himself in the scene. Big Hit saw a star in Rap Monster, and he joined their ranks in 2010. Over the next three years, the agency put together the magic combination that would become BTS.

RM is known for his introspection, intelligence (he reportedly has a 148 IQ!), and charisma. He is the driving force for the group, charging them with the responsibility of being more than just an idol group. In *BTS: Burn the Stage*, he talks about going beyond connecting with fans who just think of them as cute or catchy: "We want to listen to their stories. We want to look into their eyes and see what lives they lead and become a part of the lives of those who love us so that we can be a big help to them."

RM has led the charge in this endeavor, writing some of the band's most powerful songs, from their debut "No More Dream" (about the cookie-cutter expectations placed upon teenagers) to "21st Century Girl" (addressing women's rights) to "Spine Breaker" (taking on consumerism). He is also one of the band's most political members, who boldly breaks the idol mold to speak out about issues that concern him.

"MY SONGS HAVE MADE ME SOMEONE WHO CONSTANTLY OBSERVES SOCIETY AND WANTS TO BE A PERSON WHO CAN HAVE A BETTER, POSITIVE IMPACT ON OTHER PEOPLE."

RapMon also speaks impeccable English. All of these things make him the natural spokesperson for the group in the U.S. When asked why K-pop is finally making waves in America, he revealed the secret of BTS's success, as well as their core mission: "The world is getting smaller and smaller, and we're one of the groups that has most benefited from the new media. And music is a universal language. Thanks to fans, they're always translating our lyrics and messages…. This is the right time for K-pop [in America]."

Judging by their success so far, he may indeed be right.

VITAL STATS

Name: Kim Nam-joon

Hometown: Seoul

Birth Date: September 12, 1994

Musical Birthday Twins: Seductive soulster Barry White (1944), country music legend George Jones (1931), and music competition royalty Jennifer Hudson (1981)

Nicknames: Dance Prodigy (on account of his clumsy dancing), RapMon, God of Destruction

Childhood Dream: Becoming a security guard

Musical Influences/Dream Collaborators: Notorious B.I.G., Drake, Eminem

Hobbies/Interests: Computers, reading

Known For: His prodigious and socially conscious songwriting, work ethic, dimples

Bad Habits: He tends to lose or break things easily (Suga said he "should stay in his room for the world's peace.")

Hollywood Crush: Blake Lively

Favorite Color: Black

Favorite Food: Korean knife noodles

Favorite Number: 1

Pet Peeves/Dislikes: Tight pants

Motto: "This too shall pass."

That's So RM: "Even though youth can be beautiful, it can be short and wander off; like a shadow, it has a reckless danger to it."

FUN FACT

RM taught himself English by watching the American TV show *Friends*. His parents bought him the complete series on DVD, and he studiously watched them—first with Korean subtitles, then with English subtitles, and finally with no subtitles at all.

NO MORE MONSTERS

Until 2017, Kim Nam-joon went by the moniker Rap Monster. Now known as RM, he said he changed it because the name was seen by many as too forceful. However, he also dropped a tantalizing tidbit for ARMYs at a press call in 2017: "I don't plan to restrict myself to rapping in the future, and I didn't want to come off as too aggressive, which is why I thought about changing my name."

JIN

Jin is the band's official "visual" and the so-called handsomest member of the group. But it turns out that the moniker Worldwide Handsome is actually self-invented. "I gave myself [the name] 'Worldwide Handsome.' It's a nickname that I came up with during an interview," he told *Billboard* magazine. "Even I find it a little embarrassing to say, but many people like it, although I'm not actually worldwide handsome. Ever since our debut, I've been calling myself good-looking. You could think of it as a kind of rote teaching." In part, Jin's "handsome" image is a deflection. Turns out he's a little bit insecure, like all of us. We seldom see him wearing his glasses, even though he has a strong prescription. He is also self-conscious of his hands; he has a condition called swan neck deformity that makes his fingers curve like, well, a swan's neck.

One of the group's singers, his honey-coated vocals absolutely slay on BTS's ballads. He has a certain way of making fans feel he's performing only for them and is quite possibly the most natural of the group at *aegyo* (flirting). Because of the language barrier, you'll often see him winking and blowing kisses at the camera in English-language interviews.

Jin himself admits to being a less-than-natural dancer, but you'd never know seeing him onstage. He's

> "WIN. LOSE. I DON'T CARE, BECAUSE AT THE END OF THE DAY I STILL HAVE THIS FACE. SO WHO'S THE REAL WINNER HERE?"

confident and charismatic, and he works extra hard to make sure his moves are as crisp as his bandmates'.

Despite being the eldest of the group, the "dorm mother" is often kidded for being the band's most childish member (a unanimous consensus among the boys). Blame that on his silly sense of humor. When he's not spoiling the Bangtans with delicious suppers, he's doing silly dances or copycatting the boys.

Jin is many fans' bias because he's not afraid to show his feminine side (they don't call him the Pink Princess for nothing), because of his cheesy sense of humor, and yes, because of his strikingly handsome face!

VITAL STATS

Name: Kim Seok-jin

Hometown: Gwacheon

Birth Date: December 4, 1992

Musical Birthday Twins: Beach Boys founder and musical genius Dennis Wilson (1944) and hip-hop legend Jay-Z (1969)

Nicknames: Pink Princess, Worldwide Handsome

Childhood Dream: To become a detective

Musical Influences/Dream Collaborators: The Chainsmokers

Hobbies/Interests: Cooking and eating, photography, collecting toys

Known For: Cleanliness, culinary prowess (he once made J-Hope cry tears of joy over a bowl of seaweed soup)

Bad Habits: Snoring

Hollywood Crush: Anne Hathaway

Favorite Color: Pink

Favorite Food: Lobster, cold noodles, fried food

Favorite Number: 4

Pet Peeves/Dislikes: Leftovers

Motto: "Even when I fall and hurt myself, I keep running for my dream."

That's So Jin: "When something is delicious, it's zero calories."

FUN FACT

Jin loves Super Mario Bros. and has a huge collection of figurines. He also collects Polaroids.

EAT, JIN, EAT!

Jin's "Eat Jin" videos are the stuff of legend. Jin loves eating so much that he says no matter how tired he is, there are two words that will always get him going: "Let's eat!" Jin loves trying out new recipes, using his bandmates as guinea pigs. If he wasn't in BTS, he says he'd be a cooking show host. Ya think?

SUGA

Suga may be sweet, but he actually got his name because of his looks—specifically, his pale complexion and, according to Big Hit impresario Bang Si-hyuk, his sweet smile. The man who jokingly (or not-so-jokingly?) calls himself a genius is one of its three rappers, and its unanimous "swag master." (He's definitely got swag—and a sense of humor. When asked what his go-to pickup line was, he quipped, "Do you know BTS?" Aces!)

"Suga. Genius." Like Jin's handsomeness, it's a self-dubbed title that also happens to be true. He began his musical journey as a classical musician before turning his eye to a career in K-pop. But as he told *Elle* magazine in 2017, he has always been a writer. "I have [been] writing rhymes and lyrics, a habit since I was a kid. They are all the little minor feelings and thoughts that go through my mind. I shuffle them a year or so later, and they sometimes become great lyrics for songs." That practice seems to have paid off, as Suga has created some of the best and most brutally honest verses in all of BTS's catalog.

He has written frankly in his lyrics about his struggles with depression and also on his very personal mixtape *Min Yoongi*. ("I've denied my nature many times / My address is idol and I won't deny / The anguish that dug into my mind countless times," he writes on his

> "I WANT TO MAKE MUSIC THAT TELLS OUR STORIES. MUSIC AIMED FOR PEOPLE IN THEIR TEENS AND TWENTIES IS DISAPPEARING THESE DAYS. I BELIEVE THAT AN IDOL'S ROLE IS TO SEND OUT MESSAGES, SO I WANT TO MAKE MUSIC THAT PEOPLE CAN RELATE WITH."

"The Last.") His transparency is something that has resonated deeply with fans, many of whom credit the band with helping them through difficult times. The ARMY considers itself a support group unto itself, and the boys of BTS, especially Suga and RM, have helped bring some difficult issues—especially those people are less likely to verbalize—to the forefront.

Maybe it's his ice-cold stare, his rapper's growl, his lyrical prowess, his songwriting and producing prowess, or the smile that could melt glaciers that makes him his fans' bias. Whatever the reason, he's an integral member of the band, and one who's helped separate BTS from the pack of idol groups.

VITAL STATS

Name: Min Yoon-gi

Hometown: Daegu

Birth Date: March 9, 1993

Musical Birthday Twins: Jazz legend Ornette Coleman (1930) and rappers Chingy (1980) and Bow Wow (1987)

Nicknames: Motionless Min (because he likes to be lazy on off-days), Grandpa

Childhood Dream: Becoming an architect

Musical Influences/Dream Collaborators: Kanye West, Lupe Fiasco, Lil Wayne

Hobbies/Interests: Photography, basketball

Known For: Being the dorm father, nonstop songwriting, lethargy

Bad Habits: Nail-biting

Hollywood Crush: Scarlett Johansson

Favorite Color: White

Favorite Food: "Meat, meat, meat."

Favorite Number: 3

Pet Peeves/Dislikes: Crowds and noise (maybe he's in the wrong business?)

Motto: "Let's live while having fun."

That's So Suga: "I always wanted to nap in another country."

FUN FACT

A classically trained musician, Suga decided to change course and pursue a career in pop music after hearing Korean reggae star Stony Skunk's "Ragga Muffin" in sixth grade.

"FIRST LOVE"

For the uninitiated, the "love" in the Suga-penned "First Love" is actually not a person at all but the piano. He even accompanied himself on the piano while performing the rap onstage during the *Wings* tour.

J-HOPE

J-Hope is the band's pocketful of sunshine, the playful member who always seems to have a ready smile for his bandmates and his fans. It's fitting, then, that he's the middle member of the band in age, and he describes himself as the link between the older age line (Jin, RM, and Suga) and the younger (Jimin, V, and Jungkook). The unofficial "mood-maker," he's the one who lifts the other guys' spirits. As leader RM puts it, "If I'm fire, J-Hope is water. He's good at 'turning off' my bad habits. He's really sociable, so he's good at mixing with others and our group members."

J-Hope began as a street dancer in his native Gwangju and achieved award-winning success as a competitive dancer. Ultimately, this led to his recruitment by Big Hit and his inclusion in BTS, where he serves as the lead dancer for the band. Initially slated to be one of the singers, he became the third addition to the band's rap line instead.

He released his long-gestating mixtape, *Hope World*, in March 2018. (With only hours of eligibility before the week's album sales closed, *Hope World* not only cracked the Billboard 200 but became the highest-ever charting K-pop solo act in the chart's history.) Inspired by RM and Suga's efforts to release solo mixtapes, he wrote and produced the personal and reflective seven-song album. "I

> "IT WOULD BE HUGELY MEANINGFUL FOR ME IF I CAN BECOME, LIKE MY NAMESAKE, HOPE FOR SOMEONE IN THE WORLD."
> —TO TIME IN 2018

started dancing first, but felt I could also tell my story through my music," he told *Time*. It confronts some of the same issues that BTS tackles in its own music, including the trappings of fame and struggles to find inner peace. Unsurprisingly, like its author, *Hope World* oozes with positivity and whimsy.

Like the rest of his bandmates, he considers BTS's success to be a privilege but also a great responsibility. His goal is to keep writing and creating for the ARMY. Speaking to *Elle* in 2017, he said, "The music helped me sympathize with our young generation and also empathize with them. I'd like to create and write more music that represents them."

VITAL STATS

Name: Jung Ho-seok

Hometown: Gwangju

Birth Date: February 18, 1994

Musical Birthday Twins: The infamous Yoko Ono (1933), dancing icon John Travolta (1954), and hip-hop king Dr. Dre (1965)

Nicknames: Hobi, Sunshine

Childhood Dream: To be a "normal" college student

Musical Influences/Dream Collaborators: Benzino, A$AP Rocky

Hobbies/Interests: Movies, especially melodrama; collecting toys

Known For: Being the band's drill sergeant (translation: he's the one who nags the other guys), fastidiousness

Bad Habits: Fidgeting

Hollywood Crush: Tinashe

Favorite Color: Green

Favorite Food: All Korean food, especially kimchi

Favorite Number: 7

Pet Peeves/Dislikes: Exercising

Motto: "If you don't work hard, there won't be good results."

That's So J-Hope: "Hope is always near us, so be brave!"

FUN FACT

Wrestler John Cena posted a picture of J-Hope on his Instagram, causing the Internet to wonder whether he was a BTS stan with a Hobi bias. Turns out the band is a fan of Cena too; bandmate Jungkook even has the nickname Jeon Cena because of his wrestling prowess!

BY THE BOOK

J-Hope's *Hope World* draws its inspiration from the 1870 Jules Verne adventure classic *Twenty Thousand Leagues Under the Sea* (and J-Hope plays the lyrical role of its hero, Captain Nemo) and nods to Douglas Adams's *The Hitchhiker's Guide to the Galaxy*, among other allusions. J-Hope often uses literary references in his songwriting. Little wonder, considering he is the son of a literature teacher.

JIMIN

The man, the myth, the abs. Besides being just a pretty face, Jimin is one of the band's vocalists and dancers, the man "with the jams" and the irrepressible swag.

He is also arguably the emotional core of BTS. Whenever one of the members is struggling, Jimin seems to be there with a helping hand or a word of encouragement. (The guys unanimously agree that he's the one to go to when they need to relieve stress or need comfort or warmth.) He is empathic and openhearted, trustworthy, and loyal.

ARMYs often relate to his vulnerabilities, including his struggles with bullying and his appearance. He has been particularly candid about his past battles with his weight. That vulnerability refracts in his craft, too. When asked by *Elle* magazine what message he wanted fans to receive from BTS's music, he said, "It would be really great if our music continues to touch people. Once your heart is moved, it will develop to something better and positive."

He's a hard worker who's extremely tough on himself, and he doesn't take failure lightly. He practices his dancing exhaustively. Jimin has said that the one thing he can't live without is eyeliner, even in practice sessions. According to him, it's the magic ingredient in projecting *aegyo* and strong expressions through

> " THE FANS DON'T ASK FOR ANYTHING BACK. THEY LOVE US PURELY. THAT MAKES ME FEEL THAT I HAVE TO WORK HARDER. I WANT TO REPAY THEM."
> —IN BTS: BURN THE STAGE

dancing. He often says that his best feature is his eyes.

As bandmate J-Hope put it in an interview with *Exile* magazine, "Jimin…was born with cuteness. Another thing is that although he is younger than me, he sometimes has the attitude of a *hyung*. So I think that's his charm."

With his infectious laugh and incredible vocal range, he's an indispensable member of the group, which he considers a second family. And his warm, gooey center has won over many an ARMY.

VITAL STATS

Name: Park Ji-min

Hometown: Busan

Birth Date: October 13, 1995

Musical Birthday Twins: The incomparable Paul Simon (1941) and soulstress Ashanti (1980)

Nicknames: Dolly, Ddochi ("puppy")

Childhood Dream: He wanted to become the No. 1 swordsman in the world

Musical Influences/Dream Collaborators: Big Bang, Rain, Chris Brown, Wiz Khalifa

Hobbies/Interests: Movies, comic books, exercise

Known For: Insane work ethic (he's the one who pushes the other guys to practice when they don't want to), his eye smile, his abs

Bad Habits: Incessantly forwarding things on social media

Hollywood Crush: Rachel McAdams

Favorite Color: Light blue

Favorite Food: Meat

Favorite Number: 3

Pet Peeves/Dislikes: When adjoining tables don't line up properly (annoying!)

Motto: "Keep trying until you can't do it anymore."

That's So Jimin: "Cry as much as you like. Come into my embrace, *hyung*."

FUN FACT

Jimin's stage name was almost Baby J or Young Kid, but in the end he decided to go with his given name.

TRUE "LIE"

Jimin's solo song "Lie" from *Wings* is one of the band's most-streamed songs, proving ARMYs have much love for Jimin!

Known for his killer stare, powerful voice, and bottomless bandana collection, V is the second-youngest member of the group and its wackiest. His "4-D" personality constantly bemuses his bandmates. As RM quips, V is "10 percent genius and 90 percent idiot."

He's also BTS's unofficial social butterfly, boasting a large number of famous friends in the industry, including musicians and actors from Park Bo-gum to Park Seo-joon and Kim Min-jae. He's also a talented actor in his own right. In 2016–17, he starred in the K-drama *Hwarang*, where he won acclaim in his role as the playful but troubled young poet warrior Suk Han-sung. His bandmates agree that he's the best actor among them, and could have a career in K-drama if he wanted. (He wouldn't be the first to graduate from the K-pop ranks to the silver screen.)

His goofy and dramatic side is well-known, but he also has a flip side. His bandmates tease him about his Blank Tae moniker, but being stone-faced isn't a total invention. Just check out their recent appearance on *The Late Late Show with James Corden*. The band tried their hand at the show's popular segment "Flinch" (in which guests stand behind a Plexiglas wall while objects are hurled at them with

"BEING AN IDOL IS A LUCKY CHANCE THAT WILL ONLY COME ONCE IN A LIFETIME."
— V TO THE STAR IN 2015

great speed). Not only did V not flinch; *he didn't even move.*

He also has a tender side and is dedicated to ARMYs, especially young children. You'll often find him stopping for autographs and taking photos with his youngest fans. Sweet, sensitive, and impossibly sassy, V is many fans' bias, and an integral member of the group. (K-drama will have to wait!)

VITAL STATS

Name: Kim Tae-hyung

Hometown: Daegu

Birth Date: December 30, 1995

Musical Birthday Twins: Classical-pop mash-up mastermind Jeff Lynne (1947), pop princess Ellie Goulding (1986), and made-for-TV Monkees bandmates Mike Nesmith (1942) and Davy Jones (1945).

Nicknames: TaeTae, CVG (because his moves are perfect like a computer video game character), Blank Tae (on account of his blank expression), Gucci Boy

Childhood Dream: Becoming a professional saxophonist

Musical Influences/Dream Collaborators: Post Malone, Maroon 5

Hobbies/Interests: Animation, shopping

Known For: Eccentricities (Koreans call it "4-D")

Bad Habits: Nail-biting, yells and kicks in his sleep

Hollywood Crush: Lily Collins

Favorite Colors: Black, white, and green

Favorite Food: *Japchae* (a Korean stir-fried glass noodle dish)

Favorite Number: 10

Pet Peeves/Dislikes: Wearing shoes

Motto: "Let's live coolly and to the maximum."

That's So V: "If I have a son, I'm going to name him Chi Is Good—so he'll be Kim Chi Is Good (get it?)!"

HHcompany

STATE OF V ART

Jungkook may be the one in the band most associated with art—and his drawing talent is killer—but V just so happens to be an artistic connoisseur. When asked what his favorite things about touring America were, he answered emphatically: the Museum of Modern Art in New York and the Art Institute of Chicago.

FUN FACT

Though not the last to join, V was the last to confirm his status as a member of BTS.

JUNGKOOK

Jungkook may be the *maknae* (youngest) of the group, but he is no less hardworking than his bandmates. A triple threat—singer, dancer, and rapper (check out his chops on their "No More Dream")—Jungkook is a tireless worker who preaches the philosophy "Effort makes you. You will regret someday if you don't do your best now." And if you think that's just lip service, consider what he told *Yonhap News* in 2018: "I came to think that this year I need to do things that will help my career as a singer so I plan to quit gaming and focus on three things: I want to ace in playing the piano, foreign language, and singing." For those who know Kookie, that's pretty major indeed!

As the band's youngest member, he often reflects on how he came of age as a member of the band. To him, they are a second family, and each one of them has influenced who he has become as a man. It is a brotherhood for which he is eternally grateful. "The guys filled me in one by one. They put the scattered pieces of my puzzle back together," he said in *BTS: Burn the Stage*.

But it's not all serious reflection with Jungkook. He's probably the band's biggest prankster, and perhaps the quickest to get the guys to laugh. A certified goofball, he's also a

"WHILE YOU GUYS PARTIED, I STAYED UP LATE FOR MY DREAMS."

—FROM "WE ARE BULLETPROOF PT. 2"

voracious consumer of contemporary music, with influences as wide-ranging as G-Dragon (his ultimate idol) and Dutch duo DROELOE to Troye Sivan and Selena Gomez.

He's a little brother to all his *hyungs*, which means he sometimes gets teased by the other members but also manages to get away with a little bit more too (hence the nickname Devil Maknae). His cutie-pie looks, bottomless talent well (artistic and athletic?!), and velvety-smooth voice have won ARMYs the world over.

VITAL STATS

Name: Jeon Jung-kook

Hometown: Busan

Birth Date: September 1, 1997

Musical Birthday Twins: Crossover pop star Gloria Estefan (1957), multihyphenate Zendaya (1996)

Nicknames: Jeon Junkookie, Golden Maknae, International Playboy, Devil Maknae

Childhood Dream: Becoming a restaurant owner or tattoo artist

Musical Influences/Dream Collaborators: Big Bang's G-Dragon, Macklemore, Justin Bieber, Charlie Puth, Halsey

Hobbies/Interests: Drawing, video games, exercise

Known For: Crazy drawing ability, bunny smile

Bad Habits: Sniffling (he has rhinitis), untidiness

Hollywood Crush: He's not saying…so far

Favorite Colors: Red, black, and white

Favorite Food: Pizza, bread

Favorite Number: 1

Pet Peeves/Dislikes: When older fans call him *oppa* ("big brother"). "All of my ARMY, from now on bring your identification cards," he once quipped. Word to the wise, he'd rather be called *aegi* ("baby") than *oppa*!

Motto: "Living without passion is like being dead."

That's So Jungkook: "Let's get it!"

FUN FACT

Jungkook is probably the most athletic member of the bunch—he's a natural at everything from fishing to wrestling to archery—and motivates his *hyungs* to hit the gym.

TALENT UPON TALENT!

Jungkook draws a lot in his spare time. He's pretty humble about his talents, but the boy's got mad skills. His favorite bandmate to sketch is RM, in his trademark shades.

CHAPTER FIVE

SICK BEATS AND DEEP THOUGHTS

From the jump, BTS's music made a statement. Their bold first single, "No More Dream," sent shock waves through the K-pop ranks, heralding a musical act that was a force to be reckoned with. More specifically, they had a point of view, and they weren't afraid to take on topics that are considered taboo in Korean society and elsewhere.

Challenging the status quo is a primary focus—BTS wants to be nothing less than a change agent. "Honestly, from our standpoint, every day is stressful for our generation. It's hard to get a job, it's harder to attend college now more than ever," RM told *Billboard* magazine. "Adults need to create policies that can facilitate that overall social change. Right now, the privileged class, the upper class needs to change the way they think." Suga picked up the thought: "And this isn't just Korea, but the rest of the world. The reason why our music resonates with people around the world who are in their teens, twenties, and thirties is because of these issues."

BTS's wide-ranging scope doesn't only extend to politics. They are highly influenced by art, history, and especially literature. (A brief tour of their music videos reveals a treasure trove of influences as disparate as writers Ursula K. Le Guin and Robert Louis Stevenson, Dutch painter Breugel, and Greek mythology.) "We try to make our own BTS context," RM told *Billboard* magazine. "Maybe it's risky to bring some inspiration from novels from so long ago, but I think it paid off more. It comes through like a gift box for our fans. That's something you can't find easily from American artists."

Beyond the scope of the lyrics, BTS has striven to experiment with and expand their sound. Its seven members bring with them a multitude of strengths and musical influences, and together their music touches base with hip-hop, EDM, classical, R&B, and everything in between. With five EPs and five studio albums (three in Japanese), they've amassed a huge amount of material already…and they show no signs of stopping anytime soon.

The following discography charts BTS's releases so far, not including their three full-length Japanese-language releases, *Wake Up, Youth,* and *Face Yourself.*

DISCOGRAPHY

2 Cool 4 Skool EP
June 13, 2013

1. INTRO: 2 Cool 4 Skool (feat. DJ Friz)
2. We Are Bulletproof Pt. 2

This anthemic single serves as a rallying cry for the Bulletproof Boy Scouts, whose fan base quickly adopted "ARMY" as an extension of the metaphor.

3. SKIT: Circle Room Talk
4. No More Dream
5. Interlude
6. I Like You
7. OUTRO: Circle Room Cypher
8. Talk
9. Path

O!RUL8,2? EP
September 11, 2013

1. INTRO: O!RUL8,2?
2. N.O.

Another paean to adolescent malaise, the "N.O." in this case stands for "no offense."

3. We On
4. SKIT: R U Happy Now?
5. If I Ruled the World
6. Coffee
7. BTS Cypher Pt.1
8. Attack on Bangtan
9. Satoori Rap
10. OUTRO: Luv in Skool

***Skool Luv Affair* EP**
February 12, 2014

1. INTRO: Skool Luv Affair
2. Boy in Luv

This song was also their first nomination for No. 1 on *Inkigayo*, a breakthrough moment. They didn't win, but they did amuse fans with their music video for the single, in which all seven guys improbably fall in love with the same classmate!

3. SKIT: Soulmate
4. Where Did You Come From?
5 Just One Day
6. Tomorrow
7. BTS Cypher Pt. 2: Triptych
8. Spine Breaker
9. Jump
10. OUTRO: Propose

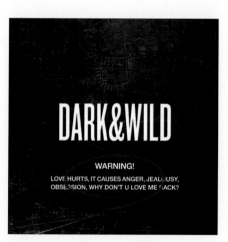

Dark & Wild
August 19, 2014

1. INTRO: What Am I to You
2. Danger
3. War of Hormone
4. Hip Hop Lover
5. Let Me Know
6. Rain
7. BTS Cypher Pt. 3: Killer (Feat. Supreme Boi)
8. INTERLUDE: What Are You Doing
9. Could You Turn Off Your Phone Please
10. Blanket Kick
11. 24/7 = Heaven

"There may be people who say that 'love stories aren't hip-hop,' but we put it in because we believe that it's an important keyword for those in their 10s and 20s," said Rap Monster in 2014.

12. Look At Me
13. 2nd Grade
14. OUTRO: Does That Make Sense?

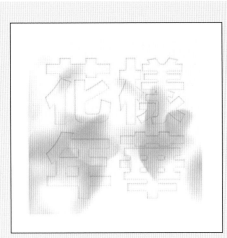

The Most Beautiful Moment in Life Pt. 1 EP
April 29, 2015

1. INTRO
2. I Need U

The boys think this is the best of their songs to listen to when you're sad. "When you're sad, you need to listen to a sadder song," Jin told Buzzfeed.

3. Hold Me Tight
4. SKIT: Expectation!
5. Dope
6. Boyz with Fun
7. Converse High
8. Move
9. OUTRO: Love Is Not Over

The Most Beautiful Moment in Life Pt. 2 EP
November 30, 2015

1. INTRO: Never Mind
2. Run

Discussing the second of what would ultimately be their *Most Beautiful Moment* trilogy, the band said, "Part one explained how youth is tiring and difficult, and it also touched on how we feel like we're always on edge. Part two will have a more adventurous and daring feel to it. That's why our title song is 'Run.'"

3. Butterfly
4. Whalien 52
5. Ma City
6. Silver Spoon
7. SKIT: One Night in a Strange City
8. Autumn Leaves
9. OUTRO: House of Cards

The Most Beautiful Moment in Life: Young Forever [May 20, 2016]
This combined issue includes remix versions of MBIML songs and also features three brand-new tracks:

1. Fire
2. Save Me
3. Young Forever

The band has said that "Save Me" is their favorite song to perform onstage.

WISE WORDS

Can you identify the songs from which the following lyrics are taken?

1. "You're a tasteless ratatouille."

2. "Miss you. Saying this makes me miss you even more."

3. "I worked all night, every day / When you were out clubbing, yeah."

4. "Don't try so hard. / It's okay to lose."

5. "Why are you shaking my heart?"

6. "Go your own way. / Even if you live a day, do something. / Put weakness away."

7. "You are great back and front. You are great head to toe."

8. "Pitiful destiny, point your finger at me."

9. "From a glance I steal a look at you / Because I'm scared to lose you if I touch you."

10. "All of this is not a coincidence. / The two of us found fate."

11. "Throw a stone at me if you've done as much as I did."

12. "We're like parallel lines / We are so different though we are both looking at the same place."

13. I changed everything for you. / But I don't know me. Who are you?

ANSWERS:

(1) "Mic Drop"; (2) "Save Me"; (3) "Dope"; (4) "Fire"; (5) "Boy in Luv"; (6) "No More Dream"; (7) "War of Hormone"; (8) "Run"; (9) "Butterfly"; (10) "DNA"; (11) "We Are Bulletproof Pt. 2"; (12) "Danger"; (13) "Fake Love"

Wings
October 10, 2016

1. INTRO: Boy Meets Evil
2. Blood, Sweat & Tears

"Blood, Sweat & Tears" was the first single to achieve an all-kill, hitting No. 1 on all eight Korean charts simultaneously. This happened in the first hour of its release, an unprecedented feat. It's fitting, considering that the single was the first that BTS explicitly dedicated as a fan song.

3. Begin
4. Lie
5. Stigma
6. First Love
7. Reflection
8. MAMA

Americans are familiar with the English-language meaning of "mama," but it also stands for Mnet Asian Music Awards, a top prize in South Korea. For the better part of two decades, the Big Three had a stranglehold on the prize, until BTS broke through in 2016. A tribute to parental support during the lean times, could the boys have also had this in mind?

9. Awake
10. Lost
11. BTS Cypher Pt. IV
12. Am I Wrong
13. 21st Century Girl
14. Two! Three! (Because We Have More Better Days)
15. INTERLUDE: Wings

Love Yourself: Her EP
September 18, 2017

1. INTRO: Serendipity
2. DNA
3. Best of Me
4. Dimple
5. Pied Piper
6. SKIT: Billboard Music Awards Speech
7. Mic Drop
8. Go, Go

"It isn't a BTS album if there isn't a track criticizing society," Suga said of the song exploring the emptiness of materialism.

9. OUTRO: Her
10. SKIT: Hesitation & Fear
11. Sea

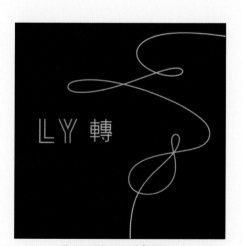

Love Yourself: Tear
May 18, 2018

1. INTRO: Singularity
2. Fake Love

More like *mad* love! This song cracked the Billboard top 10 in June 2018 to become BTS's highest-charting single—and the highest ever for a K-pop group.

3. The Truth Untold
4. 134340
5. Paradise
6. Love Maze
7. Magic Shop
8. Airplane Pt. 2
9. Anpanman
10. So What
11. OUTRO: Tear

CHAPTER SIX

THE ARMY WANTS YOU— BASIC TRAINING

By now you've had an introduction to the wonderful world of Bangtan, but so many pleasures still await you. Have you checked out their YouTube channel, BangtanTV? And what about all their music videos? You gotta go way back to their very first song, "No More Dream," to see 'em all. And of course there's Twitter, Facebook, Instagram…the message boards and fan forums…the reality series…their Bangtan Bombs and all that old footage from their musical competitions…their mixtapes and collaborations with other artists…. Yes, being a fan of BTS is the gift that keeps on giving, and the sensational seven are only one mouse click away.

But first, why don't we brush up on our Korean, shall we? The Modern Language Association says that there was a 45 percent increase in Korean language students among American universities in recent years. Could K-pop be the reason? Here are a few essential Korean words and phrases every K-pop fan should know.

CAN YOU TALK THE TALK?

aegyo: Acting flirtatious or cutesy, it's especially associated with the flirtatious onstage behavior of idol groups. Jimin's got it in spades with his eye smile.

aigoo: Not to be confused with the above, it's an interjection used in surprise, frustration, or chastisement meaning, basically, "Oops."

an moo: Choreography. It's universally considered an essential element of any idol group.

assa: Woo-hoo!

be peu: Like "BFF," it's an abbreviation meaning best friend.

bi dam: The most attractive member in a group.

chingu: Friend.

choom: Dance.

daebak: Awesome.

dongsaeng: Meaning younger brother or sister, it can be used to refer to anyone younger than oneself.

ganji: Stylish, trendy, fashionable—your everyday ordinary swag.

gayo: Another name for K-pop.

gomawo: Thank you.

gwiyomi: Slang term for someone adorable or cute, often a child.

haeng syo: An informal way to say good-bye, roughly translating to "Peace out."

hoobae: Meaning "junior," it's a respectful term of address for someone younger/more inexperienced than you.

hul: Next time you want to type "I can't even…" try this instead, roughly meaning "whoa."

hyung: Older brother, but can be used to refer to a close friend as well.

jebal: Please.

jon jal: Incredibly good-looking, when referring to a male—as in, "My, is Jimin *jon jal*!"

king wang jjang: If you love BTS infinity squared, try this phrase on for size. It doesn't get any more superlative than this, meaning the absolute best.

maknae: Youngest member of a group, as in Jungkookie.

maum: Emotions, or heart. Warning: a maum can be stolen!

mi nam: A handsome guy.

nam chin: Boyfriend.

omo: Oh, my!

oppa: Older brother, or any male older than oneself.

saesang: An overly obsessive fan…but not in a good way.

sa rang hae: I love you.

selca: Selfie.

shim koong: Like the feeling you might get seeing your first BTS concert, it means your heart is beating a mile a minute.

sunbae: Meaning senior, it's an honorific that members of BTS would use to address, say, Rain.

yeo chin: Girlfriend.

Okay, so you think you're a BTS expert? Test your mettle on the following quizzes to find out if you're certified ARMY.

TEST YOUR BTS IQ

1. Which members comprise the *maknae* line?

2. What was BTS's first single?

3. Who is known as the father of the band?

4. Who is the official visual of the band?

5. Which of the following is the full Korean name for BTS? (a) *Bangtan Songdan*; (b) *Bangtan Songjeam*; (c) *Bangtan Sonyeondan*; (d) *Bangtan Songyeodan*.

6. Which of the following is *not* a variation of BTS's name? (a) Bulletproof Boy Scouts; (b) Burn the Stage; (c) Beyond the Scene; (d) Bangtan Boys.

7. True or False: Suga didn't start writing songs until joining BTS.

8. Who's the only member of the band who has his own room in the dorm?

9. BTS's EP *Love Yourself: Tear* hit No. 1 on the iTunes chart in how many countries? (a) 36; (b) 42; (c) 60; (d) 73.

10. Which charity did BTS partner with for the Love Yourself campaign?

11. Which of the following was not a possible name for the band before they settled on Bangtan Boys? (a) Big Kids; (b) Bang Bang; (c) Young Nation.

12. Which BTS artists have released solo mixtapes?

13. Which of the following classic books was the inspiration for the BTS album *Wings*? (a) James Joyce's *Ulysses*; (b) J.D. Salinger's *The Catcher in the Rye*; (c) Hermann Hesse's *Demian*; (d) Joseph Heller's *Catch-22*.

14. Which American artist has *not* collaborated with BTS? (a) Kesha; (b) Wale; (c) Desiigner; (d) Fall Out Boy.

15. What is SOPE-ME?

16. Who is RM's favorite *Friends* character? (a) Ross; (b) Rachel; (c) Joey; (d) Chandler.

17. Which is BTS's best-selling album to date?

18. On which program did BTS make its American television debut?

19. Which is not the title of a BTS song? (a) "Young Forever"; (b) "Just One Day"; (c) "Run"; (d) "Dark and Wild."

20. True or false: BTS's American fan base is most densely populated in Hawaii, California, and northern Wisconsin.

WHO SAID IT?

"Teamwork makes dream work."

"All trouble starts with me…and ends with me."

"Don't be trapped in someone else's dreams."

"Look up and we're all looking at the same sky."

"I wish I could come here with my girlfriend, but I don't have one."

"That seagull over there has a girlfriend, so how come I can't get one?"

"English is not a barrier when you're as cute as me."

"I'm very loser."

"Hannah Montana says nobody's perfect, but here I am."

"Kill them with success and bury them with a smile."

"I cut off my bangs accidentally. I thought my life ended."

"I think it's the most sunlight I've got in nearly five years."

"I'm your hope, I'm your angel."

"I hope you know your limits well, but don't stay within those limits. Overcome the limits each day."

"I'm extremely unmotivated."

"*Jimin i pabo.*"

NAME THE BANGTAN BOY

1. This member gets a twitch in his eye whenever he becomes hungry, which is often.
2. This member used the stage name Gloss before changing to his current moniker.
3. Which member is most often teased for his height?
4. Which member was supposed to have been in EXO?
5. Whose stage name was almost Seagull?
6. This member used the stage name Runcha Randa.
7. This member has performed under the stage name Agust D.
8. His stage name stands for the word "victory."
9. Which member of BTS almost dropped out before their debut?
10. This member is the most likely to receive a Korean Drama Award someday.
11. This member has kept a daily diary for many years.
12. This member has a secret talent for tumbling.
13. This member was initially to become a vocalist for the band before being put in the rap line.
14. This member studied dancing in the U.S.

FINAL QUESTION: GEOGRAPHY

Okay, so now that you've learned everything you ever wanted to know about BTS, here comes the real question. Where will you see them next? The Bangtan Boys just announced the first round of dates for their international *Love Yourself* world tour, selling out dates as fast as tickets have gone on sale. (Tickets for the L.A. show immediately went on resale sites for upward of $1,000 apiece before a fourth night was added at the 20,000-plus-seat arena.) Maybe you're one of the lucky ones to score an audience with your idol? *Hwaiting!* (That's K-pop speak for go slay.)

August 25	Olympic Stadium	Seoul
August 26	Olympic Stadium	Seoul
September 5	Staples Center	Los Angeles
September 6	Staples Center	Los Angeles
September 8	Staples Center	Los Angeles
September 9	Staples Center	Los Angeles
September 12	Oracle Arena	Oakland
September 15	Forth Worth Convention Center	Fort Worth, Texas
September 16	Forth Worth Convention Center	Fort Worth, Texas
September 20	First Ontario Centre	Hamilton, Ontario
September 22	First Ontario Centre	Hamilton, Ontario
September 23	First Ontario Centre	Hamilton, Ontario
September 28	Prudential Center	Newark, New Jersey
September 29	Prudential Center	Newark, New Jersey
October 2	United Center	Chicago
October 3	United Center	Chicago
October 9	The O2 Arena	London
October 10	The O2 Arena	London
October 13	Ziggo Dome	Amsterdam
October 16	Mercedes-Benz Arena	Berlin
October 17	Mercedes-Benz Arena	Berlin
October 19	Accorhotels Arena	Paris
October 20	Accorhotels Arena	Paris

ANSWER KEY

Test Your BTS IQ

1. Jimin, V, Jungkook
2. "No More Dream"
3. Suga—he handles manual labor and fixes things around the dorm.
4. Jin
5. C
6. B: *Beyond the Scene* is the title of their 2018 YouTube Red docuseries.
7. False: after learning classical composition in middle school, he began writing songs nearly every day.
8. Jungkook: he won the privilege by winning rock/paper/scissors.
9. D
10. UNICEF
11. B
12. RM, Suga, and J-Hope
13. C
14. A
15. A rap-comedy duo composed of Suga and J-Hope
16. D
17. *Love Yourself: Her*
18. The American Music Awards broadcast
19. D: *Dark and Wild* is the name of their 2014 album
20. Believe it or not, that's true!

Who Said It?

"Teamwork..." (RM)
"All trouble...." (V)
"Don't be trapped..." (V)
"Look up..." (RM)
"I wish..." (Jin)
"That seagull…" (Suga)
"English..." (Jimin)
"I'm very..." (J-Hope)
"Hannah Montana..." (Jin)
"Kill them..." (RM)
"I cut..." (V)
"I think..." (Suga)
"I'm your hope..." (J-Hope, natch)
"I hope you know..." (RM)
"I'm extremely..." (Suga)
"Jimin i pabo." (V)

Name the Bangtan Boy

1. Jin
2. Suga
3. Jimin
4. Jin
5. Jungkook—a nod to his coastal hometown of Busan
6. RM
7. Suga
8. V
9. J-Hope
10. V
11. RM
12. Jimin
13. J-Hope
14. Jungkook